The Apple Speaks

THE DREAMSEEKER POETRY SERIES

Books in the DreamSeeker Poetry Series, intended to make available fine writing by Anabaptist-related poets, are published by Cascadia Publishing House under the DreamSeeker Books imprint and often copublished with Herald Press. Cascadia oversees content of these poetry collections in collaboration with the DreamSeeker Poetry Series Editor Jeff Gundy (Jean Janzen volumes 1-4) as well as in consultation with its Editorial Council and the authors themselves.

1. On the Cross
   By Dallas Wiebe, 2005
2. I Saw God Dancing
   By Cheryl Denise, 2005
3. Evening Chore
   By Shari Wagner, 2005
4. Where We Start
   By Debra Gingerich, 2007
5. The Coat Is Thin
   By Leonard Neufeldt
6. Miracle Temple
   By Esther Stenson
7. Storage Issues
   By Suzanne Miller
8. Face to Face
   By Julie Cadwallader-Staub
9. What's in the Blood
   By Cheryl Denise
10. The Apple Speaks
    By Becca J. R. Lachman

Also worth noting are two poetry collections that would likely have been included in the series had it been in existence then:
1. Empty Room with Light
   By Ann Hostetler, 2002
2. A Liturgy for Stones
   By David Wright, 2003

The Apple Speaks

poems by
Becca J. R. Lachman

DreamSeeker Poetry Series, Volume 10

DreamSeeker Books
TELFORD, PENNSYLVANIA

an imprint of
Cascadia Publishing House LLC

Cascadia Publishing House orders, information, reprint permissions:
contact@CascadiaPublishingHouse.com
1-215-723-9125
126 Klingerman Road, Telford PA 18969
www.CascadiaPublishingHouse.com

The Apple Speaks
Copyright © 2012 by Becca J. R. Lachman
All rights reserved
DreamSeeker Books is an imprint of Cascadia Publishing House LLC
Library of Congress Catalog Number: 2011028273
ISBN 13: 978-1-931038-93-5; ISBN 10: 1-931038-93-7
Book design by Cascadia Publishing House
Cover design by Gwen M. Stamm

The paper used in this publication is recycled and meets the
minimum requirements of American National Standard for Information
Sciences—Permanence of Paper for Printed Library Materials, ANSI Z39.48-1984.1984

Versions of poems in this collection have appeared in various outlets.
For a complete listing, see Acknowledgments section, back of book.

Library of Congress Cataloguing-in-Publication Data
Lachman, Becca J. R., 1980-
 The apple speaks / Becca J.R. Lachman.
  p. cm. -- (DreamSeeker poetry series ; v. 10)
 Summary: "Lachman's poetry offers rare glimpses into contemporary Swiss Mennonite life and engages issues of community, negotiating daily life, family, humanitarianism, race and gender, Mennonite life, and more" --Provided by publisher.
 ISBN-13: 978-1-931038-93-5 (trade pbk. : alk. paper)
 ISBN-10: 1-931038-93-7 (trade pbk. : alk. paper)
 1. Mennonites--Poetry. I. Title.
 PS3612.A337A67 2012
 811'.6--dc22
                                       2011028273

*For humanitarian workers around the globe ...
but more for the families who love them.*

Contents

I

Preludes • 13

II

Portrait of a Grandmother, 1949 • 21
What My Parents Gave Me • 22
An Anabaptist Learns Tai Chi • 23
You Wanted This World • 26
Can You Remember the Smell of Alfalfa on Your Hands? • 27
Talking Poetry with an Amish Bishop • 28
Sermon 1: No Stoplight in This Tourist Town • 30
 2: The World from Up Here • 32
 3: And Yet, And Yet • 34
Saving the Springhouse • 36
Poem Written Four Hours from Home • 37
When Red Rushes Up • 39
"He Steps into the Sky" • 41
Earth-Smelling Secrets • 43
A Confessional Carry-In • 45
Reading Plath at a National Mennonite Convention • 47

III

A Father's Calling • 51
Old Order • 52
Psalm to a Simple Supper • 54
Will There Be Pianos in Africa? • 56
What Should I Wear for the Journey? • 57

My Mother as Minister/ of Music • 58
Ascension • 60
Liberian Man, Survivor • 62
Uprising • 64
Ava, German for "Bird" • 66
My Father Eats McDonalds • 67
Girl on Somalia Drive • 68
A Hundred Ways to Kill a Rooster • 70
Our Own Kind of Advent • 72
Reverence • 74

IV

Method • 77
No Anchoress • 79
Mozart Hands • 81
Liftable Garden • 83
The Piano in Barrancabarmeja • 84
Blood Tonic • 86
The Apple Speaks • 88
New Marriage, a Barn Raising • 90

Notes and Dedications   92
Acknowledgments   93
The Author   94

PRELUDES

ɸ

No one else stopped open-
mouthed to listen,
but the tree in the park
was singing that warm day

in November, full of wrens
small as men's thumbs. It couldn't
help itself, leaves not dropped
or collected like the others, still

a gold bouquet of open umbrellas
hiding tiny cymbals. I left
before music could flee.

ɸ

Farmers harvested early, as much
as they could before the crow-
cloud found them.

Which scared the boy most:
his father's shaking hands or how
the sky shifted before diving
into cornfields?

He watched from tractor cockpit,
shit hitting the windshield in white-
purple fireworks. After awhile, only
thickening stain.

He couldn't see wings settle: mad choir
in the cedars. Like locusts in the Bible,
Jehovah sent birds.

ϕ

For three days last spring, rustling
in the chimney—an exhausted
starling. We peered at each other
through the woodstove's glass door.

"We thought you were dead," I kept on
telling it. "You've been so quiet…"

Instructions for Trapped
Pair of Wings:
{1} Pull down all window shades.
{2} Throw front door open.
{3} Focus on that frame of light.
{4} Urge the bird to fly straight.
{5} Exhale when it hears you: one perfect arrow
     of ash and feathers.
{6} Hold your breath; it sings. You

will not need a translator.

ϕ

The old
woman
bought
a deserted
farmhouse
with a yellow
pine winding
up from the
basement,
through dining
room, and out
decaying roof,
nests in higher
branches. She
sobbed when
men came with
axes and chain-
saws, salvaged
the trunk for
lovely blonde
floors. Now
she walks upon
what knew
the house first.

ϕ

Matisse said everyone has a tree
inside them. Some root through
the impossible, flee towards fire.
Faint angles of light—and then—
such music. We thought

you were dead, we keep on saying.
You've been so quiet.

You've been so still.

PORTRAIT OF A GRANDMOTHER, 1949

A great lid covers this place, she thinks while dressing in the dark

that first Sunday. Outside, the jerseys form a wandering

bell choir. She is thankful for the noise.

In soft light, the white dress makes her feel like a ghost. *Or*

a bride, she makes herself think. *A bride.* She smoothes down its collar,

she enters the kitchen, tries to help with bread or coffee. *Out!*

remains her almost-mother's answer.

At the service, her face burns but has no choice

but to follow other women. Across the aisle,

men greet with holy kisses. No one speaks. They stand for

    the first hymn. She, the white mark among

hundreds of dresses, all of them black. No one warned her

that morning at breakfast. Not even him.

WHAT MY PARENTS GAVE ME

The tremor of his voice box
coaxed me from dreams made heavy
by the hymn's drone.
I stared down at slanting wooden
floorboards, the black church shoes of strangers,
held my breath and listened to my
father's honeyed tenor,
listened with a sudden flash
of protection, *He is mine.*

Clinging to his torso like a
morning glory vine, my warm
four-year-old face pressed
to the prickly curve of his neck, I heard
where the music began—
a trickle inside, a rocket of breath—
and I remember even
then wanting to touch that place, to
cup it in my fingers.

I'd watch my mother's monarch hands
from where I lay half under the grand piano's
stretched belly, my own
palm atop her cold, bare toes
as she pumped the stubborn pedals.

AN ANABAPTIST LEARNS TAI CHI

In emptied rooms I crave
high notes; my first instinct,
to sing. Yes, this is what
my body has been taught:
music, an offering—
music is God breathing.

   * * *

We are not here to look
in each other's faces.
No one speaks except our
teacher. These are the rules
and for them, I'm grateful.

Our lungs supposed to fill
with warm honey, slow as
"being" is its deaf self.
Don't you know where you come

from? my body demands.
I'm arching back, reaching
toward ceiling. *Body*

means "church," means "work." Prayers are
things kept solid, spoken.

   * * *

Hard to find my balance

in a room of gathered
slowing down... Body? Let me
love this limb, my neck, a
shoulder, mindful. Arms flail
for a trusted center,
any worth resting on.

From across the quiet,
the teacher watches, one
black eyebrow arched. Fidget,
doing "snake creeps down."
Wobble, trying "windmill"

or when turning my hands
into cranes so tender,
touching both shoulders with
finger-beaks. Slow, sacred

dancing I can let my-
self do. Breath forgets, won't
stay in the body. Be

    * * *

baptized again, sigh deep.
Ask to repeat this sad

striving. Oh notice: the

spirit ladled out, then
cradled in. I have learned
other moves: "turn cheek" or
"push the anger down." My
mouth quick to disown them,
but bones remember, then

muscles follow; they tell
the body I'll get back
to it later. But here,
"falling water" comes with
two raised arms: my own. *Look,*

between breaths, I ask them—
these open cloud hands, lungs
light with honey. With birds
on both shoulders, I sing—

Are we saved?...Are we saved?

YOU WANTED THIS WORLD

On my birthday, the orchard smells of apple
cider, fruit soft under our shoes.
*You were here in less
than an hour,* my mother tells me
in her kitchen. Speaking of labor pains, she braids
thick slabs of New Year's dough
to rise up with afternoon sun.

You wanted this world.

We smile at the thought of me, dancing against
her stomach to be freed. Butterflies—
gray and yellow and white—dash at purple asters
like living salt and pepper. The last heirloom
tomatoes hang, heavy hearts now shaded
by the skeletons of sunflowers.

These things are always present
on this day, every year so constant. It is me
who comes back with questions about worth,
unable to sleep in my childhood
room. *So many moments in life
like this*, when change is as certain
as the morning, when spent apples
bleed into the ground untasted, and your body
takes the time to remember its birth.

CAN YOU REMEMBER THE SMELL OF ALFALFA ON YOUR HANDS?

The fields still take my breath away.
It isn't like I forget them in the city
or discover something better
in cur-le-cuing sidewalks or the eager
pull of skylines at night. I don't notice
them at first, as I'm bringing in suitcases
or petting the dog. But when

I'm on my way to the bulk food store,
when the purples and blues of sudden
winter drip down past the lull of the hills,
my body and mind remember each
other, the car still racing towards
shelves of dried fruits, honey, a whole
room stacked with cheese.

The only car on gravel roads, I speed
because I am used to motion; to beat a rush
that does not exist in a place where cows
and tourists outnumber any other. Here, the stars
still speak at night. Once I step from behind
the wheel, into the smell of living
acres, there is nothing between me
and skies holding snow that spill like paint
-brush water toward the fields that raised me.

TALKING POETRY WITH AN AMISH BISHOP

The world knows your quiet; I know
your harvest of words. It has been a year

since we stood in your back field, recited bits of
Berry and Frost. You have no doubt

harnessed the draft horses hundreds of times,
sat on your porch with a library of books

after long seasons of listening, arguing
with the earth. I remember

your feet—it sounds silly, yes, but
I'd never met an Amishman in *sandals*—

and the swift June rain chasing us under
two maples. You gave me your barn coat, and the sky

threw its body down—we almost had to shout—*What do you
think of the president these days? How is the market for

soybeans, jerseys?* Water gathered in the rows you'd been plowing,
spilled from your hat brim; I looked down at mud-flecked ankles.

Can we really write out how this world aches, how the heart will
never stop planting its questions? Why we are born into

stillness, spend the rest of our days filling it in with any-
thing? The team horses stood, steaming statues—I remember

their quiet presence too. *Have you changed that stanza,
the one where you're out picking blackberries?* Have I

changed my life after that day in your field, since running
to dodge lightning, waving to your sons, then backing

my car down the drive? Have I paused long enough to gather my-
                 self from the quiet in the land?

SERMONS
1: NO STOPLIGHT IN THIS TOURIST TOWN

Those who are not among us bring
their cameras and their children. They leave
what's heavy on their hearts for a morning, a day.

Those who are not among us bring ready
billfolds, pay for bentwood rockers and log cabin
quilts. So easy to buy
an hour of quiet. It is not surprising
on Sunday mornings to see a car with windows open

stopped where the road dips between Salem and
Sonnenberg. God is a cappella
on the seventh day. Hymn crosses
hymn between these two churches, and music carries
off centuries of feuding (This the visitors
don't know; it is rarely talked of now—how coffins
were plucked like red beets in the middle
of the night, away from the mother church.)

What does our martyr family think as we
sit back, barter our quiet to the world, pretend
that we are holy, different? *Six friends ended their lives in*
great joy, and those that saw them burn went and
penned a hymn, the first letter of each verse
replacing the names of the dead.

Do *we* feel warm when breathing deep to offer up
our harmony? Do we think of them
as verses change? And what *would* they say, after

watching us join the frontlines, deadlines, the weight
of such wealth: *Burn us, bake us, drown us,
world—yet in the end, make us yours?*

2: THE WORLD FROM UP HERE

From the pulpit, congregations
mimic those Kansas fields,
the ones we're supposed
to have visited
already: wind-swept-
predictable, they wait
for the coming
of a crop they're sure
to recognize.

* * *

For years,
I have carried
my body
like something
I couldn't quite
shake, like someone
I dreaded
meeting in public.

For I've never known
what to say to her
in private, have never
sat—just the two of us—
on the front porch
before a storm
or a bleeding winter
sunset, because

she's not the kind
you're taught to want
to bring home.

*   * *

Finally, I am loving
what I carry. On paper,
the world drips
off of shoulders.
*Body, I need
you! Body, I sing
you onto the page!*

*   * *

From the pulpit,
the world
spreads, even
its legs. And I open
my mouth to tell it,
   You're beautiful.

3: AND YET, AND YET

I forget that the balm can be quiet,
left to the unspoken

coils. Our wounds can heal through
something other than speech
or prayer. Silence that could rend,

forgiven instead by simple actions:
rhubarb sugared, a touch on the shoulder,
the verse of some prodigal hymn

relearning the breathy shape of soul.
Come. Just listen to soil and root

on a walk that lets us, too, be holy.
Some would call this uncomfortable,
ever-healing *grace,* that lavender

hummingbird nesting in ribcages, no matter
if we welcome it or not. Sometimes

we think it's just a tremble of the heart,
a deep catch of involuntary breath. Birds
remember flight, try to hover above

something, even when in cages, even cages
of rib. We are taught, not by a spoken lesson

or binding book, but by watching those before us.
How to breathe in private as if welcoming
the world, as if taking it inside us…We remember

places we've never known. Our mouths can
shut; they can and still be beautiful.

SAVING THE SPRINGHOUSE

Yesterday, we watched an Amish funeral
from our moving car, just as the sunset
dyed the white barn pink. A slow
line of ants, carrying
their dead. We passed at a distance,
couldn't make out faces in the midst
of that long living postcard. A tourist
in my own hometown, I wanted to join
them, ease into their silence like floating
on the surface of deep water.

Not long after, Grandpa saved
the springhouse, shifted 1840s sand-
stone floor, reinforced walls to hold
his childhood together. Inside,
his father's glass insulators still
line shelves tall as the men

who built them; one life's collection
of sorted color. In a building no longer
visited daily, sun slants— and blue
moves on to amber.

A farmer I never knew
once stood in this parade of hardtack
light. At the end of a day,
after working the earth, surely
       he wanted
a ladle of water.

POEM WRITTEN FOUR HOURS FROM HOME

Cleave—1. to split with a sharp instrument...along a natural line of division
    2. to pierce or penetrate
    3. to make one's way
    4. to be faithful
      —American Heritage Dictionary

iv.

What dreams are ploughed under when we cleave ourselves
to the land of our fathers, mothers, martyred soil wealthy with roots!

iii.

Twenty years ago now we stumbled across the dumping ground
of our ancestors: bits of blue china accidentally dropped, glass
insulators split down the middle; rusted shovel heads, hammers, wire-
rimmed frames at the bottom of a creek bank. For two sisters,
it was Egypt, this watery unearthing. Pieces of people we'd never
meet but could hold, rub clean in our hands.

ii.

The Amish have built their dawdis for centuries, houses that birth
houses to keep all loved ones close. From the road, it's often obvious
where new additions have sprung: sudden porches, chimneys, back
screen doors, new rooms for newer roles. To keep his only daughter

iv.

near, my grandfather gave open fields as wedding gifts.
A piece of the farm: such a generous father, such a quiet yoke.
Our dawdi was fashioned from trees, streams, the path
through high corn to Grandma's kitchen.

i.

Now I do not know where to start my own building, when
to pound the first nails—onto what, onto whom?

WHEN RED RUSHES UP

*"True humility is neither thinking too highly of one's self
nor thinking too little of one's self, but rather
not thinking of one's self at all."*
—Amish proverb

"What does a woman want?"
—Sigmund Freud

Silence is what scares
me most. You see, I come from
a long line of martyrs
who gave up their lives to be
heard. Some women
were drowned at night in secret,
their testimonies grown
too powerful. Even with tongues
screwed tightly down, a mother's body
still begged for crowds to admire
      and fear such faith.

Burned, baked, stretched and smothered,
they made their public offerings, turned back
on splitting ice to save
their executioners
in order to sit at their heavenly
banquet. Or to follow a man
across the country, raise
his children, cook his potatoes
just the way he likes them.
      I come from

persecution set ghosting
in lungs and feet so heavy black-
purple, it's impossible to boil it
out of us. Look at the way
some tongues are still
        missing.

I carry these two apples with me
daily: cheeks that still expect me
to stand in ready flames with all
that is said or asking for it —or, even
worse—*un*said, since I might be taken
as prideful or clinging or my mother's
mother, Eve's ready
hand. All these things and more
rush to my face like fire. Shameful
ripening. Ripening,
mirrored: the silence
for which I'm piling up
                the stones.

"HE STEPS INTO THE SKY"

Crouching at the side hatch of the roaring Ford Trimotor plane, a young man peers into a thick column of smoke 1,000 feet below. He waits for the spotter's signal, and for the pilot to cut the engines. Then he steps into the sky. It's summer 1944 and thousands of Americans his age are parachuting onto smoky World War II battlefields in Europe, Africa and Asia. This man's war, though, is not against foreign troops. He's a Montana smokejumper and a conscientious objector to that other war. . . .

—smokejumpers.com

Montana is shaped by flames
in the summer breath of 1945. You are called
yellowbellied, told to eat at other tables,
your quiet faith suddenly
visible as sickness. Twelve thousand refuse
to fight. Some end up at work camps or as
human rats in government labs.

Three hundred are smokejumpers.

*Conscientious objectors won't
sour my men,* you hear again
and again, right before
you step into the sky, step ironically
from military planes, into the battle between
flame and wood.

So used to farming from sunup till dark, you will
not admit exhaustion— there are landing rolls
to perfect, fire lines to dig. There is land
to be shaped, far away from Midwestern

cornfields. And right before your foot hits air
and the burning earth rushes up, you can't help
but be reminded

of the way your chest felt when you stole
that first warm kiss.
Or the way your shoulders shivered
with baptismal water. You

can't help but hear again,
Be still and know. . . .

EARTH-SMELLING SECRETS

My grandfather found wild
  mushrooms in the woods. He'd pick
thick finger-bodies, all for
  special suppers, fill cover-
all pockets, then tell no one:
  an old farmer deserves his
earth-smelling secrets. But then,

he forgot where normally
  they siren up from earthy
dark; he scoured the under-
  brush, grumbling. It started, in
fact, with glasses (his best pair)
  left on a forest boulder
or somewhere near the trailhead…

We joked that a rabbit was
  reading much better. For years,
it was laughter for forgive-
  able things. Now, he forgets
that he shouldn't walk alone.
  Hefting his wishbone frame from
recliner—alarms, people

come in one mighty *swoosh,* sharp
  inhaled prayers. All around him
are farmers in rooms, farmers
  who know the earth and so would
rather fall there on the ground's
  firm stillness, than here on floors

that shine strange. On some evenings,

he recalls where the mushrooms
   now wait, marked by his hand with
an old tractor tire. They're
   still on a hillside of May
apple umbrellas, there where
   he fell years ago but could
not get back up, rolled toward

trees, braced knot body against
   them. He has forgotten this.
Tonight, he's talking mushrooms
   in Swiss phrases he's not used
since youth, and he whispers like
   the shy boy who's just revealed
the most precious of secrets.

A CONFESSIONAL CARRY-IN

Nothing like a dinner party where every guest
is self-invited. Sure, some say they were forced
to attend, but still they sway in, self-ignited.

The clock strikes one. Plath is ravenous filing
past the casseroles. "My heart's in that one,"
Ginsberg points to an old crock-pot that's

just half full. A table for each of us— the help
must've figured we'd only want to talk
to the self. (But the whole world knows:

to confess to no one is, of course, our version
of hell.) New to the party, I can tell what
they're thinking as they crowd round my plate

sneaking bites of dessert: "We only want
the damaged details." Sexton smiles, Lowell
smothers wet burps. "Tell us your most shame-

ful secret!" Some of the women are eating blue pie.
Olds holds a wishbone with Berryman. "Yes,
describe your sex life as a *Mennonite*."

But what can I give them that will be enough? What
good will it do to put onto paper doubt's great
heaving silence or lovers lost? Will writing them out

make the present safer? I clear my throat and ask
for water. We wonder aloud about recipes.
Roethke chokes on an olive when I finally blurt

that "From now on, I won't write about me."
They nod, turn away, having heard it before.
Out of their own mouths they've spit this same key.

Some roll their eyes and continue to chatter,
argue over whose life is most sour, most sweet.

READING PLATH
AT A NATIONAL MENNONITE CONVENTION

There is too much movement in the world. They have
    Come to find their center: it is often singing.
Thousands and thousands, girls in braids and men

Who laugh in public spaces. Give us our trespasses
    So we may cup them, fireflies caught. Our debtors
Against us, we kiss cheek-to-cheek. Hollow

Be our bones. Women known by their fathers, husbands
    ('Stutz Ivan's Ruth). I am Hank's Rebecca and would not
Change it. She would love it here or run in terror: so many women

Who stick their silly heads in ovens daily. The dark thought flashes—
    Orange then green—before fluted crusts emerge, women
With something whole or burning. Many things

Can cool their thoughts: after soft rains, weeding; empty
    Rooms; not waiting; psalms read aloud to early light. They are
Not as simple as I write them, they are not

Flat or white as this page. They spin to still
    Taught oceans of doing. Under soft skin, bodies will
One foot into wilderness. Some answer. Here she could

Take notes for hours, might ask covered heads
    That turn why their words are calm water, cruel
Bulbs. Planted, she would no doubt call the church

Old Bearded. Would she then advise, "Girls with *gentle talk*
    And mild obeying never bend away from home". . . ? Wait,
Sylvia. Those here are early to everything, eager

To save, the first to reach disaster. Breathe and be filled, you just
    Might tell them. They would offer you the same
  Spirit sewn into hem or propped, scarecrowed in garden.

A FATHER'S CALLING

I choose to think of him outside the station wagon
pulled over by the freeway at dawn. He has jumped
the ditch, is freeing a collie. Its hind legs dangle high
in barbed wire. His thumb has split during struggle;
blood trickles straight to wrist.

Beyond the fence: new corn, a farmhouse toy-like
in the distance. And I am the six-year-old waking
in her seat, convinced, at first, of her abandonment;
then wondering if the dog will lash out—worse—
that it can't be freed. Either way, I remain

the daughter
of a man who will not pass this by.

OLD ORDER

Nothing new: in my childhood sin sang out
in color, and we always named it black. Fear too
made clear its inky mark. A town, one
thousand faces pale as cheese.

One settler carved a chair for his pale God, dressed
all in white for Second Comings when Christ would
finally sit and rest. He carved his other visions too: spiraling
fire, talking doves. The chair sits in our museum, never used.

We never thought we'd be the type to stare
at a black Amish boy in line at the Fire-
men's barbeque. Swiss lips kept in
those hot and silent questions.

Even the soles of their feet were hot, those lovely
West African daughters poured into long-
sleeved cape dresses. A covering got them
in and fed. The black ink did the rest.

They fear the albino inked in white, the girl pursued
by witch doctors. Her eyes worth a full wagon
of rice. Her heart intact? A year of schooling.
At night, she hides in sheets black as their hair.

Black trees on the page, old words still root us. The poet—
you know the one—who carried hungry lilies, dressed all
in white? We hold her hymn-rhythms in secret, word-minnows
wriggling, black ink rising. White words of fire and God,

nothing new. Sin-minnows rise singing; we catch them
in our clear blue stream. A town, marked and lovely.
A thousand faces tilted towards sun, and a high
wooden chair built for vision, waiting on the dove.

PSALM TO A SIMPLE SUPPER

We came from our comfort to serve you
ham and canned green beans, cornbread and
black coffee. We came
in our used cars, passed you
making your way against winter
gusts and the steady tug of pride.
In the old church basement we'd look at you
through different windows, from distance
guarded.

We sing for you in the sanctuary some
old familiar hymns, have time
to study the unwashed face, the aged
curve of spine, decades of guilt
burrowed into forehead, stories
lodged between shoulder blades.

I am a good person, I tell myself as my
heart skips a beat when, after your
belly is full and fingers are once again
pink, you move to embrace me
much like a happy grandfather would. You are
a boy of seventeen as you
squeeze my cheek to yours. You are not
judging me, while I am taking in
your rough, dirty stubble,
your mismatched wardrobe, the way your arms
remind me of a clinging scarecrow. You are calling me
Sweetheart, gently patting my hair, and I never
ask your name. Somehow you know that

we came from our comfort to give
and go back quickly
into our worlds where smiles are not
toothless, where suppers are seldom
simple. Somehow you know
and forgive.

WILL THERE BE PIANOS IN AFRICA?

I come home late, just days before their flight, to mama singing with her fingers. The tune, loud and running—not even perfect— but the song itself hasn't changed. We remind ourselves of things that last: father belts high notes beside her, throws back his head— a bird calling to each lyric like flight. The white scales are sour, giving in to summer damp, but the piano will not be tuned again.

Soon they will eat supper cooked
over charcoal, lie down in pyramids
of mosquito netting. Africa calls to them,
away from this well-lit living
room, from my mother's mahogany baby
grand. Will her fingers trill
in her sleep? Upon her sheets, will they drum out
ragtime, hymns, or Mozart?

Tonight, my parents sing with no tears, without knowing they have an audience. I listen just outside the door,
I will stay and do what they have taught:
how to sing a line like a silver circle, how to end
a phrase like coming home. When I can no longer
talk to life without you, *Mother*,
        don't you worry—I will sing.

WHAT SHOULD I WEAR FOR THE JOURNEY?

Ridiculous, really, to fear these miles
soon to divide the maps
that are so hoped for. Change
will come in deep, rich furrows,
in the way every living thing
defies its own stillness, reaches
to lead itself
forward: a root
for its thirst, a stem for its sky, thread
for the very top of a loom.

Drape your love around me
like a sari. You pick the colors—green
for my eyes, gold thread for my hair—
the pattern, even the length. Cloth,
the same as grace, once
stitched by needles of bone.

Children are made to outgrow
their child bones, but mine refuse
to be forgotten; they are
hot and blue as stars. Sitting
at the loom. Together, a pattern
comes faster. Spool. Needle.
Thread. Daughter. Hands. Open,
daughter. Thread. When you are
gone, I will try to remember.

MY MOTHER AS MINISTER OF MUSIC

Sometimes I think that African music
was planted like an acorn in the heart
of my white mother. Gourd-bellied sahsahs, thumb
pianos, djembes—they'd always sat in corners
waiting. In the Mennonite farmlands of Ohio,

the need was always there
for a loud and pulsing rhythm that would drag her
from straight Protestant benches and into
church aisles 6,000 miles from head coverings,
pursed lips, and elders. Dancing joy-filled to the pulpit,
she would sing out in languages
she'd never known. Before

Africa wooed her, her
church choir belted out spirituals
but always sounded bored or desperate, singing
with as much movement as they could muster
without offending, accustomed to a cappella
harmonies, the tender blending
of human voices.

In Africa, God is deaf—the singers must
shout louder! One voice over another! And my mother
wails. My mother juts her arms into
the rafters. From that acorn in her heart,
she grows winding tiara branches, white and sharp
and sun-bleached, longing for sky.

The Kisii choir swells. She teaches them
Handel's "Hallelujah Chorus"
by rote, one part at a time. They teach her
how to sing loud and long from the very beginning
of the self, from the part that God heard
long before we ever felt
its sprouting.

ASCENSION

[God] cared as much as on the Air
A Bird—had stamped her foot—
And cried "Give Me"—
            -Emily Dickinson

I have seen a bird tremble in hands
almost praying, its perfect, wild
winging captured and cupped.
I have seen it crescendo out
of the hands, free into trees
but knew—and know now—it would never
be the same (nothing
ever is when it's seen
its own heart flutter)

Why do you stand looking
into the sky? becomes the voice
in the trees, folding, un-
folding the hands, the wings. The bird
somewhere shudders. My head
is always bowed.

See, I have engraved you
on the palms of my hands, the voice comes
and goes. But this is no
comfort: heaven's hand
pressing down always—heaven's fist
squeezing both the holy and the world
right out of us.
There was a time I thought trees

were the oldest parts of God keeping
the earth so wholly together. I believed
in my body that could climb God's hands,
believed in the birds that swooped
from barn rafter to branches with language
as delicate as their bones. I believed in them
because in heaven, I would also
crescendo. Now, now the body
wants home.

Branches hang suspended
before thunderstorms and snowfall.
There were things the sky told the birds, the girl,
the trees and their
beautiful reaching.

But now, by the end of the day,
the girl stands under trees, her face tipped
towards sky. Swallows
crouch in the hands of God. The grip
whispers
again and again just how far
down the ground really is.

And by the end of the day,
        they believe.

LIBERIAN MAN, SURVIVOR

"He killed my ma, he killed my pa, but I will vote for him anyway!"
—1997 presidential election campaign slogan for Charles Taylor

The bell was safe, the bell was
there when the troops started firing.
    Come, crawl back into this womb,
it called, and so I hid, curled my body
high into its palm, my screams
against the thick of its throat. Below, the bodies
dropped, first heavy like falling boughs, then softer
as layers grew thick, sweet with life still
trying hard to linger.

Life pried me out: my body still
breathing, my wife outside scratching
for my arms. The doors were opened,
the church was silent, sun-filled. On
any other morning, it would have meant prayer.

Now, I go to the market and see them.
Risen from the sanctuary floor, they sell me
pineapple and peppers, ask about my daughters,
jabber on and on. They follow me home,
smoke after dinner. They argue and bicker,
then expect me to talk.

I *want* to tell them something—anything, really. But
nothing can be said, not to death. And if I break with the quiet,
will the ringing start? Will I find
the bell empty?

The silence
is what saved me. After the last bullet, it was only
mine to hear.

UPRISING

I am preparing for your resurrection.
On my twenty-fifth birthday, you call from your continent to mine
just to tell me of the lopsided cupcakes made in my honor, baked in
a new outside oven (Really, a spent refrigerator that now
houses flame.)

For fourteen months, you have been this same voice: a repeated,
four-minute conversation, a soft silver
place I keep in my belly. There are people in the
streets, you tell me over emails, people coming
to the city to hold their rallies, marches; you can no longer
drive anywhere. Monrovia's pulsing, its sky
smells constantly of storm. Here in Ohio I also

wait for the uprising: your actual fingers, your real
breath in the room. For fourteen months I have
regrown myself, rethought my routines, shaken dirt
from bony roots, gotten through sometimes by not
remembering you. Now, the stone

begins to roll away. Over coffee and toast, walking
to work, my stomach twists into
your name. Just yesterday, you wrote
of neighbor children snatched in the night
for sacrifice. It is too hard to believe—
the witch coming to your door, then sensing that
holy armor. It is too much to be given— these
bodies filled with war, even after back roads have absorbed

their dead. Today, I passed what must have been one
hundred turkey vultures, circling over State Street, and I
thought of you in your rainy season. *I'm already
packed*, you warbled a month ago, wanting to pretend we were
out together: *We have potato chips, glasses of White Zinfandel. We can
talk for hours, can see and touch our smiles…* Mother,

for fourteen months you have been picked from my bones.
And now, I must welcome you back from the earth. I must do this,
knowing you will return to the thunderclouds and children
and to streets holding war. Too soon, you will ask
to be that thin silver place, and I must simply
let you.

AVA, GERMAN FOR "BIRD"

"Lit-tle red-bird in the tree, in the tree, in the tree,
Lit-tle red-bird in the tree, sing a song for me…"
-children's song lyric

I. A memory comes to me:
    *We are four and seven, sisters playing
hospital. We are singing nurses (just
as they should be). It is right
after breakfast; the whole day
    shimmers. Dolls are tucked
into couch corners. How easily
we switch from playing nurse to*
   playing mother.
*Our plastic children are perfect and
tender. We name their illnesses, then
take them away.*

II. Men are crying in the waiting room; I think
one of you has died. The doctors have cautioned
there is no time to waste; make sure to talk
to the minister. Our parents are finally reached
in Africa (in four days, they would have
stood here). Being prepped for the birthing
surgery, a nurse hands you
the phone: mother
to daughter, daughter
to mother, mothers
and daughters
trying to get out—you are all there,
listening.

MY FATHER EATS MCDONALDS

Again and again the hand (gold-banded) dips into perfectly
salted fries. The other grasps vanilla shake like it's all that is
left in the world. This happied meal, this reunion with sweet
catsup often filled your Ohio-dreaming-into-humid-West-African-
waking (the dogs and roosters fight early). How
tender! your wife whispers, holding up the half-moon of a burger
like it's a secret you mustn't let on that you know. There is silent,
worshipful swallowing. Nodding. The rescue of more fries.

> On long trips into the bush, your team of medics would have no
> choice but to buy dinner from the side of the road. Personally,
> you'd hope for pineapple eaten like candy or peanut bread and
> roasted corn, hot pepper sauce to burn down louder hunger.

But now (even now) you cannot forget a certain
future dinner sitting with you in the back seat for hours
of smelly meditation. "Bush meat" means
any number of things, and the monkey still stares
at you, unblinking, even here in your red plastic
booth. Its hand refuses to stay at the bottom
of the soup bowl.

After the stomach finally settles (two Big Macs and shake
in one sitting), you remember where you've been. Where
you'll soon choose to return. You have taught it all your life, this
clunking guilt: that those who have the most must give
up the most, bite-by-bite, spoonful-by-spoonful. It is the way
we starve ourselves that is important.

GIRL ON SOMALIA DRIVE

I am not prepared to see her.

We have the car windows closed
so no arm can reach
in, see what white skin has
to offer, partly to block out the burning

fumes. Diesel trucks in front of us mimic
boats on stormy water (Children have been lost
in the mahogany puddles
of rainy season
potholes.) The streets pulse
with vendors, ex-child
soldiers, long dogs with teats dragging
in the dirt. We crawl past
a slaughterhouse, the Coca Cola factory, a truck-bed
packed with workers singing of the Promised Land.

We are some sort of horrible royalty

here from America, the real Promised
Land that sent its slaves
back to the blade of Africa. We are tied
to the others outside our car windows
by blood and sweat, quiet
greed. Men suck their teeth
at my mother and me, a way of getting
our attention. They watch us pass with longing, money
signs, and awe. Babies cry—to them,

we are ghosts.
I have learned to be overly interested in my shoes.

When I do look up this day, a flash of white
draws me to her blue-black
body, its flawless curves. We are, perhaps,
the same
age. We look into
each other's
eyes, five seconds
at the most,
though much of her face
is missing. Where nose and
cheeks should be, only scars
turned the color
of my hand.

I want to tell her, six years
later, that she still steps into
my vision, stares back unblinking

to let me know what she has seen.

A HUNDRED WAYS TO KILL A ROOSTER

Just wait, they will get hungry,
my mother promises at breakfast
after I complain. *Your luxury is to be annoyed
by little things.* In early morning,
when our neighbors rise at four
to bake sweet foolah bread to sell
on Tubman Boulevard, only rainy season
at its worst can keep him from prying
open the world.

I've watched him closely
outside the screened window of the room
where I take my bucket bath: he runs stiffly
through puddles, green-gold feathers
ducking through legs of children to escape
the sudden mean downpours, to crow happily
inside instead.

Across the street, the Nancy Doe
market slowly spurts to life, its war-damaged
buildings filled with dried fish and fufu, children
selling mayonnaise jars of gasoline, pushing
wheelbarrows of flip-flops, children who shake
shy heads "no" when we ask them
for a picture. No one needs
another soul stolen here. Even from the market,
I make out the rooster's cackle.

I get to know him

well; by the end of a month,
I am sure he sounds different
when announcing a storm
blowing in off ELWA beach (like a trumpet
that's been trampled). As he becomes that grandfather clock
villain-laughing-out each quarter hour,
I wish for him instead a slow death
by fire ants. Even

the over-sized avocado pits at lunch
begin to seem like the perfect artillery.

I dream of other weapons I could hurl
over the compound wall, past the highest layer
of broken glass and wire. Always
the generous American, I try
to think of things his struggling owners
could *use:* two shoes? a dictionary? a pot
or a pan?

Liberia's Independence Day—a morning
that brings loud singing and strangers
to our door smiling, asking for the gifts they know
we can give, and my last sweaty
morning in Africa—I wait
for his usual green-and-gold boasting.
How fitting that silence is all
that comes over the
compound's sturdy wall; *it means,* my mother smiles,
a fuller thing.

OUR OWN KIND OF ADVENT

Five months after Africa, my father finally digs out
the familiar music for the familiar
version of himself to play
on his recorders from Heidelberg.

Growing up, there were endless nights
like this: me finishing the day's
dishes, my mother with sore feet
in a bath, father drawn to what can be answered

only by pitch and rhythm. Wexford Carol, What Child
is This? spin into rooms now settling
into the recognizable. Tonight,
the prodigals, the fatted calf. The longest
night of the year.

Earlier in the car, my mother cried
at the sight of electric candles in windows, even
at giant, inflatable santas, confessed,

> You will never know how homesick
> we were a year ago. Now, home

is not that shunned idea   banned
to an African apartment closet   in boxes
of letters, photos, a curl of your
first granddaughter's hair, German
recorders swelling with heat, all
hidden to protect you there
in your giving. When do you get to

stop? Calming oceans
by the spoonful   open hands
become the things   that leave you restless.
In the rooms of your house

your family still waits for you—
the people known
before The Call. Instead

you appear burning   like that star
above Bethlehem   or the seraphs
in the Old Testament,   tangible signs
of something glorious and   horrible
that God is about to do . . .

REVERENCE

The deep night brings the heavy question
Whoo? spat at the air, breaking
snowed stillness. Two owls duetting, talons tearing at
roof tiles, wake my parents' unsuspecting
sleep. The Great Horns
are right above them, dueling for a winter mate with
clashing beaks, unearthly wails. And my parents, finally
warmer under quilts, listen like children.

Come morning, my father will find the battle's loser
dead and frozen in the apple orchard, its beak slightly bloodied,
esophagus ripped clean away, but its body
untouched. Golden eyeballs iced
over, wings half raised, as if determined to die
guarding something, anything—half in and out of flight.

My father will prop the dead owl on the woodpile,
try to decide what to do with such a specimen, energized
by the touch of his hands on talons, wings: so many things
that man is not supposed to touch.

Jays and crows will circle in blue and black "S"s,
will dive for the bird feeder when they realize
the hunter is dead.

IV

METHOD

—In memory of David Citino (1947-2005)

Always use the stairs. Eat chocolate
when analyzing poetry. Memorize
a favorite verse, the bite of syllables,
heaviness and lightness left
in shoes or back pockets. Kiss the world
hard; the hard world hides
children and Italy, long
embraces, fight songs, powerful
chatter. Find them. Find time to write
what you want from this world over and over,
Over coffee or in 5 a.m. emails, repeat aloud
that line—*Do you really want
the break just there?*—and surprise yourself. Embarrass
the day with what you've been thinking.

So often the heart of it reveals itself quite
accidentally, when we try
to explain, talk about something other
than what's actually on paper. And (Do I
even have to say it?) talk
only after listening. See beauty, even
in Cleveland alleys, muddy rivers, fields
of alfalfa. Teach beauty, teach
holding words + letting them go (Please note: this
takes time. First, go and find them, dry them as leaves
between wax paper, then hold them toward light at various
times of day). Teach only what you know or think
you have loved. Write what you live but also

long for. Finally, write nothing
on a bright October morning. Follow
the Appalachian Highway, the Hocking
River, follow them until
you feel you are now ready to claim that end
stop, a description of the trees; until you feel
that you are willing
to write them down for good.

NO ANCHORESS

Tell me, Emily, that you were scared
that the world was out
to eat up your punctuation,
or that you were simply the luckiest
of any of us, walled up like an Amherst
anchoress, your whitest secret being
that you sold the self to what you loved.

Tell me that since you questioned
God, he came to woo more often, grateful
for the challenge or just a simple wink.
Tell me that you've read over
the slouching shoulders of high school
students, how you've flicked
the backs of heads when they could not
feel the fire
in all that darted language.

Better yet, remind me how,
by holy reincarnation, you now work
at the local bakery to pay all the bills, mixing
dry ingredients with oils and egg
at 4 in the morning, the constant knead.
Assure us that after your shift, you rush
homeward seven blocks to a rented
room alive with winging words, trailing flour
like exotic sand, a-buzz from daily
lattes or the constant lightning
of strangers' glances.
You can still write with thoughts of crashing

markets and future children and dirty
dishes and high hell and heaven, all coming
as cacophonictic flashes in the pan—
why couldn't you? Stanzas surely frame
those small barred windows on
sticky notes, cover the fridge, fill up
kitchen drawers, always retelling,
redazzling themselves.

MOZART HANDS

My mother tells me I have
"Mozart hands." A music teacher,
she should know. "Such little hands
for so much you want to do," she coos
over a new composition fit to my
fingers, the chorus a round red ring.
        My panty-hosed piano teacher in college
        shows me how to stretch cartilage
        between fingers, thumb. In smooth moon arcs,
        I'm supposed to want to widen my reach.
        "*Make* yourself play it," I hear her repeat.
So swallow-boned, my hands have learned nothing
except to want a little more, resting on wrists
that threaten by day's end to bend, break, take
away the crescendo or the poem's best ending
because they are hollow or just so damn tired.
        I order my wedding dress based
        on new measurements: size four
        on top, a twelve on the bottom. This
        can't be right, or am I such a tilting treble
        clef, meant to stand so gruelingly
        grounded, hipped to things I cannot
        hold in place for long?
I can barely reach an octave on the piano
keyboard, making Rachmaninoff even more
Romantic because I could never truly
have him. And such is life; the simplified version
performed in quiet practice rooms, or only
for audiences made up of family and the dog.
        In my early twenties, in a distant city, I duck

into a Tiffany's to get my real ring size,
just in case. Just for me, curious. Barely a 4½.
"A dainty finger," the jeweler quips. I'll let you
believe it, I think to myself, jutting hands
like something stolen back into my pockets.
Years later, my husband will have Mozart
memorized, play it some mornings while he's
waiting for the bathroom, like it's normal
for perfect cadences to come before granola
or even birdsong. He tunes pianos. He listens
to whatever intervals I play. And he squeezes
my hand, which does not break.

LIFTABLE GARDEN

In the middle of the night, we rush barely
dressed, to save our young tomatoes, the sugar
snap peas just beginning to curl. Away
from hail and thunder, we lug their water-logged
containers under awning, squinting through sideways

rain. In heavy seconds we are soaked to the skin, jump
back to dry land with boldness, laugh loudly to imagine what
our neighbors would think if they saw us, so desperate to save
our first little-movable-barely-greened
garden, dashing nakedly about among falling
branches in leaf-choked wind. This is how I want

to remember you: hair dripping and smile
wide, your body young and asking, soil between
your toes. A new husband, a new wife, awakened
by the world. I want to keep you
like this, and me so willing to jump
between the time lightning strikes and the thunder
answers—so ready and eager
to save something we've made.

THE PIANO IN BARRANCABERMEJA

There is one public piano in Barrancabermeja, and my composer
husband has never seen it. On our one-year anniversary, he swears
he will eat cake with his too-sweet Colombian coffee. He swears to
love me more than other things that ask for his return:
scrubby, gray-green jungle or paramilitary youth
with gold-capped molars, the dirty waters of Rio Magdalena.

Peace needs husbands from everywhere, even
boys from coal country, even composers. Midst the gunfire
and missing, mine wants to get in the way, to give as much
to beat-up ploughshares as soldiers give to battle. He learns
not to flinch. He shines up his Spanish, learns to shout,
"I'm watching!" the way a Colombian would say it
to the eyes in the forest or the planes that drop
their fire onto fields.

I will be here that anniversary, in July's hot mouth with my own
cake heart, wanting the sound of his heels keeping the beat
upstairs, his music spouting from splayed-open fingers.

Barrancabermeja's piano has a legend
like this: once a year, two chosen hands reach out
to sing an audience silent. Its ivory keys become the words
that form a single sentence, different for each member
in the crowd. Some hear, "There's no forgiveness" when
the music's finally opened. Others are given, "I should have
had more sons" at the end of a lilting cadence. "Where she is,
she can hear this" hovers over one woman sitting in the back,
just when crescendos shake through wooden floorboards.

For the rest of the year, the Steinway waits in the city library's
tired belly. Alleyway salsa or *vallenato* must rock
Barranca back to sleep. And the green rushes up
in the country. And the river valleys glow. *Familias* run, petroleum
shifts, and red clay is packed deep into the ground, earth you claim
looks so much like ours. Here, where you raised two beds

before leaving for raspberries. Here, where I will drink
my morning tea, then lie on your side of the covers, our bed
like the top of an unopened grand playing out, "Come home.
Come home."

BLOOD TONIC

Without you, the kittens only
have me on which to scratch
their love. Hand, wrist, ankles—
hardly ever blood—skin
heals in tough pink skids.

We are happiest today crouched
in dirt near potatoes: kittens
batting chicken wire or jumping
ribboned onion tops. My voice,
their newest mother.

The fence you built leans out
but holds us. Small harvests
ripen, mostly red. Baskets fill
with things torn open, pulled
loose, cut close. I miss

your rooted weight beside me.
No stopping rain or heat; each
morning, new things to carry
inside, eat quickly.

My fingers later will be sweet
purple with beets, red plumes
on the cutting board, one glass
plate piled with their bitter-
spot leaves.

My body, too, can bleed. Tonight it will
remember—surprised, even
grateful—that it is mine for
the summer, all mine. No

mother, not really, not yet.

THE APPLE SPEAKS

I did not ask
for this garden. It's all rushed green
and waiting for a man who won't
be here to see its full bearing.
He's left me for God.

He brought it in truckloads
of dirt, chose what would be planted. Now
I flick off small beetles. Ripening,
my waiting, a fat green tomato he'll never
salt. What I love most: those called

to far-off places. They hear the same voice
three times in the night. I am
no war widow. My pining's not for missing

soldiers, something to blazon on bumpers.
At least then, I could carry *Enough!*
Bring them home. In nightmares,

my husband stands at a checkpoint, turning
another cheek. My parents leave again
for other children's sake, cross bullet-holed

bridges, fall to waters that don't part.
Here, my mouth shows its teeth
to those who ask how I'm doing

alone. We are the silent ones left to carry
their mail inside. Absence, a coat
to unbutton. We pray to a soft wing that answers
rewards will be great
and the harvest, it's ready. I wonder

about the taste of late
summer apples. Unclenching, red
skin finally splits
to tell no one in particular.

NEW MARRIAGE, A BARN RAISING

What it all comes down to: unpaid community
labor gathered 'round the first post and best

beam. O impossible ark, built to be
grounded, raised by well-beloved

hands. Attendance mandatory by risk
of shunning. Even children have tools

to fetch and sharpen. Some rough hands
welcome only because they must be. Now

young men in rib-rafters who once just
watched from hillsides call out to women

for water or a smile. What grins up squinting is
certainty they long for: childhood, the sturdier

step on ground they know, even a body not
one's own. Each acts out the expected, assembles

despite any previous plans. Walls go up slow
but sturdy. To shoo away debt. To shade out

loneliness. Secured for storage and readied
for life. A framework, in the end, they will not

own, these worn-out masses. And still they come,
hands willing. Still they gather when new couples

settle. Or after a fire. Or following a flood. O urgent
love, come back and see this time next year what stands

NOTES AND DEDICATIONS

"No Stoplight in This Tourist Town" uses a direct quote from *The Martyr's Mirror* (also known as *The Bloody Theatre*). A popular book in Mennonite homes, it consists of more than four thousand accounts of those who were baptized as adults, practiced nonresistance, and died for their faith.

"Talking Poetry with an Amish Bishop" is for David Kline.

"He Steps into the Sky" is for Ivan Amstutz.

"A Confessional Carry-In" includes the names of prominent "confessional" poets and uses the colloquial term *carry-in* instead of *potluck*.

"Reading Plath at a National Mennonite Convention" contains fragments from the poems of Sylvia Plath (see italicized text).

"Old Order" alludes to "White" Jonas Stutzman, the first Amish settler in Holmes County, Ohio. Since we should always "hold Christ above us," he built a large chair for the Second Coming, which he believed would occur in 1853. The chair can still be viewed at the Amish and Mennonite Heritage Center.

"Ascension" references Acts 1:11 and Isaiah 49:15-16.

"Ava, German for 'Bird'" is for Sarah Nussbaum.

"Liberian Man, Survivor" refers to a massacre inside Monrovia's St. Peter Lutheran Church in 1990, where hundreds of people perished. Today, many claim to have been the only survivor.

"No Anchoress": An "anchoress" was a woman who often lived in a door-less cell connected to a church; she served a monastic life sheltered from society. The anchoress lifestyle reached its height during the Middle Ages; many anchoresses were "given" to the church by their families. "Emily" in this poem refers to Emily Dickinson, who famously chose a reclusive lifestyle.

"The Piano in Barrancabermeja" is for Christian Peacemaker Teams (CPT) in Colombia.

ACKNOWLEDGMENTS

Poems in this manuscript previously appeared in the following publications, sometimes in slightly altered form:

Rhubarb: A Magazine of New Mennonite Art and Writing, Octave Magazine, Red Thread Gold Thread: The Poet's Voice, The Mennonite, Dreamseeker Magazine, Center for Mennonite Writing Online Journal, Poetsagainstthewar.com, Tongue Screws and Testimonies: Poems, Stories, and Essays Inspired by the Martyrs Mirror (Herald Press, 2010), and *"Songs from the Spring-House"* (2004 Florence Kahn Memorial Chapbook Award, Verdure Publications).

SPECIAL THANKS TO—

The people of Kidron, Ohio, and Monrovia, Liberia—whose stories are ever evolving; they have changed me.

Michael Lachman, Marilyn and Hank Rossiter—for their uncommon love.

Alison Prindle, Angie Estes, Jim Gorman, Susan Kinsolving, Timothy Liu, Major Jackson, Mark Halliday, Sharmila Voorakkara, and Jeff Gundy—for their mentorship, for their literary citizenship.

THE AUTHOR

Becca J. R. Lachman was raised in the Swiss village of Kidron, Ohio, most famous for its picturesque farmland and a world-renowned non-electric hardware store. She learned to sing and lead hymns from her mother, a long time minister of music. Her first original musical was produced during her 8th grade year.

Becca has been a student of the arts all her life and is happiest when sitting in front of a piano and microphone. Her choral music is available through The Lorenz Corporation's Heritage Press. In 2004, she graduated with a B.A. in creative writing and music composition from Otterbein University. After Mennonite Voluntary Service in Seattle, Becca earned her M.A. in English from Ohio University and her M.F.A. in Literature and Writing from the Bennington Writing Seminars.

Like most Mennonites, the poet grew up with alternative service as an important cornerstone. Her grandfather was a conscientious objector smokejumper during World War II, and her parents served as missionaries in Liberia, West Africa. Now married to a Christian Peacemaker Teams reservist and fellow musician, Becca teaches in the English department at Ohio University in Athens. She is still a long-distance member of Kidron Mennonite Church.

www.ingramcontent.com/pod-product-compliance
Lightning Source LLC
Chambersburg PA
CBHW022108040426
42451CB00007B/173